A+ books

Go Go Global

FOOD of the WORLD

by Nancy Loewen and Paula Skelley

raintree

a Capstone company — publishers for children

Around the world, all the day through,

ice cream: England

we **lick** and **nibble**, **chomp** and **chew**.

udon noodles: Japan

We **slurp** and

munch and

gobble too!

Morning's here, so open **wide!**

traditional breakfast: England

It's **time** to put some **breakfast** inside.

Eggs or porridge,

huevos rancheros: Mexico

rommegrot: Norway

spreads on toast ...

Vegemite spread: Australia

waffles

Belgium

or falafel –

Egypt

which do you like most?

What will you **munch** when it's **time** for **lunch?**

Thailand

Skewered meats in **spicy sauce,**

8

a **hot dog** in a **bun** ...

empanadas,

Argentina

a slice of pizza ...

Italy

munching lunch is fun!

Creatures on sticks,

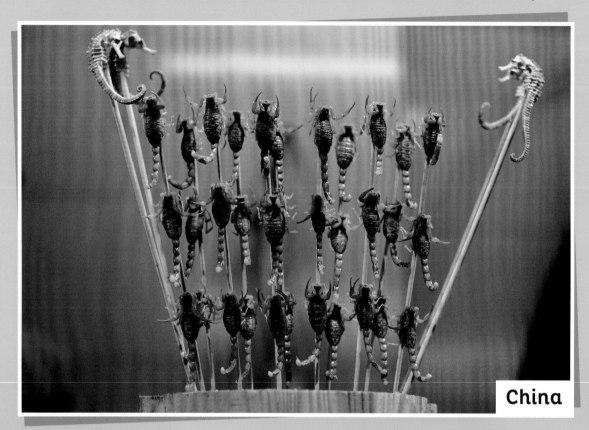

China

Australia

Colombia

Ireland

grubs, chocolate and crisps ...

snack
time
has us

spring rolls: Vietnam

Lady Finger bananas: Thailand

licking our
lips.

tortilla chips and salsa: Mexico

The **day** has gone by.
It's **getting late.**

chicken and lamb curries: India

Time for **dinner** –
fill your **plate!**

14

aguadito: Peru

Sip some **soup** or **sample** **sushi.**

Japan

Bite a **burger** ...

United States

Morocco

or **kebab.**

Pass the poutine

Canada

and **paella.**

Spain

Thank you, dinner was **fab!**

Celebration meals set the **mood.**

roast turkey (for Thanksgiving): United States

Special days call for special **food**.

Doughnuts

fried and **filled** with **jam,**

tangyuan (for Winter Solstice Festival): China

sufganiyot (for Hanukkah): Israel

dumplings

soft and **tender,**

golden threads

of **sugar** and **egg**

foy thong cake (for weddings): Thailand

for **gatherings**
we'll **remember.**

Meat and corn steamed in leaves,

hallacas (for Christmas): Venezuela

"herring under a fur coat" (for New Year's Eve): Russia

fish topped off with veggies ...

a **pretty** pudding,

Christmas pudding (for Christmas): England

26

a tall ring cake –

food is how we celebrate.

kransekake (for weddings): Norway

Mmm... delicious.

Would you like **more?**

So many **wonderful foods** to **explore!**

chickpeas: Nigeria

layered rice cake with chicken: Iran

watermelon: Israel

beetroot soup: Ukraine

bird's nest baklava: Turkey

meat and vegetables with flatbread: Ethiopia

29

NORTH
AMERICA

Canada

*United
States*

Mexico

SOUTH
AMERICA

Venezuela

Colombia

Peru

Argentina

Norway

EUROPE

Ireland

England

Belgium

Ukraine

Spain

Italy

Turkey

Israel

Iran

Morocco

Egypt

Nigeria

Ethiopia

AFRICA

ANTARCTICA

Russia

ASIA

China

Japan

India

Thailand

Vietnam

AUSTRALIA

Australia

GLOSSARY

celebrate do something fun on a special day

empanada fried or baked pastry usually stuffed with meat

falafel spicy mixture of ground vegetables (such as chickpeas or fava beans) formed into balls or patties and then fried

grub soft, thick, worm-like larva of certain beetles and other insects

kebab cubes of meat cooked on a stick

paella dish of rice, meat, seafood and vegetables

porridge creamy, hot cereal

poutine chips topped with gravy and cheese

skewered stuck on a stick

sushi cold rice with raw seafood

GO GO GLOBAL DISCUSSION QUESTIONS

1. Name three foods in this book that people around the world may eat for dinner.

2. Look at the foods for special days. Explain how they are different from everyday foods. What makes them special?

Raintree is an imprint of Capstone Global Library Limited, a company incorporated in England and Wales having its registered office at 7 Pilgrim Street, London, EC4V 6LB – Registered company number: 6695582

www.raintree.co.uk
myorders@raintree.co.uk

Edited by Jill Kalz
Designed by Juliette Peters
Picture research by Tracy Cummins
Production by Tori Abraham
Printed and bound in China.

ISBN 978 1 474 70369 7
19 18 17 16 15
10 9 8 7 6 5 4 3 2 1

British Library Cataloguing in Publication Data
A full catalogue record for this book is available from the British Library.

Acknowledgements
Alamy: Gastromedia, 24; Shutterstock: Alex Hubenov, 14, Amornism, Cover BR, baibaz, 4, Baloncici, 28 Top, Blend Images, 2, Bochkarev Photography, 20, bonchan, 11, 17, Boris-B, 22 Left, Brent Hofacker, 6, 7, 18, cobraphotography, 5 TL, David P. Smith, 13 Bottom, deepblue-photographer, 1, Dereje, 29 Bottom, dolphfyn, 22 Right, Dr Ajay Kumar Singh, 28 BR, e2dan, 15 Top, gulserinak1955, 29 TL, HLPhoto, Cover TL, 10, 19,28 BL, jabiru, 5 Bottom, Jack.Q, 3, Karl Allgaeuer, Cover TR, Cover BL, kavring, 5 TR, Kenneth Sponsler, 9, leocalvett, Cover, 1 (globe), Lesya Dolyuk, 26, Lisovskaya Natalia, 12 BR, m00osfoto, 12 Top, Olga Dmitrieva, 8, 16, Rakov Studio, 15 Bottom, senlektomyum, 13 Top, Settawat Udom, 13 Middle, skyfish, Cover Back, Stawek, 30 Bottom, Timolina, 25, topnatthapon, 23, V. Belov, 27, Vankad, 29 TR, Zurijeta, 12 Middle; SuperStock: NHPA, 12 BL.

Every effort has been made to contact copyright holders of material reproduced in this book. Any omissions will be rectified in subsequent printings if notice is given to the publisher.

BOOKS

Eat (Say What You See), Rebecca Rissman (Raintree, 2014)

Food From Farms (World of Farming), Nancy Dickmann (Raintree, 2011)

Vegetables (Healthy Eating), Nancy Dickmann (Raintree, 2011)

WEBSITES

www.bbc.co.uk/education/topics/z672pv4/videos/1
Watch these videos about food and farming around the world.

www.letsgetcooking.org.uk/lets-get-cooking-around-the-world
Ask an adult to help you try out some of these recipes from around the world.